FABER NEW POETS 7

Sam Riviere

———

faber and faber

First published in 2010
by Faber and Faber Ltd
Bloomsbury House
74–77 Great Russell Street
London WC1B 3DA

Typeset by Faber & Faber Ltd
Printed in England by T. J. International Ltd, Padstow, Cornwall

ACKNOWLEDGEMENTS

Thanks to Jack Underwood, George Szirtes, Lavinia Greenlaw,
Tim Cockburn, Matthew Gregory, Nathan Hamilton, Emily Hill,
Jo Shapcott, Andrew Motion, the Society of Authors for
an Eric Gregory Award, the Arts and Humanities Research Council,
the editors of *Bedford Square 2*, *Pen Pusher* and *Poetry London*
where some of these poems have been published, and to my family.

A CIP record for this book
is available from the British Library

ISBN 978-0-571-25001-1

2 4 6 8 10 9 7 5 3 1

Contents

Poems

When he met her it was as if he could see
his poems moving around below her skin
like fish in an aquarium. To attract them
he tapped the glass of the tank –
some were pretty big fish. They loomed
close, shadowing her face like a birthmark.
He saw their luminous scales, the frills
of their fins, their mouths, fat and defenceless,
without natural predators, begging
to be caught, mounted and nailed to the wall.

The Kiss

the more she thought
the more she thought
she'd keep it to herself – he'd never know
exactly how it happened (*she* didn't know)
and he'd see replays of her face
opening and reaching towards *his* face
and know a truth
that was a type of truth,
then he'd try
to fill in details, and try
to understand
(he wouldn't understand)
and end up with an image more real
than the event itself was real,
and so telling him would hurt,
but it wouldn't be the truth that hurt
but the words
(the words
would come out wrong) then his man's mind
would take over, the image in his mind
would be there, and really it was selfish
to tell him, she was being selfish,
and so she arranged the food
on the plates, taking care the different food
didn't touch, no she'd keep from saying,
she'd keep saying
to herself that *it was nothing*
and *it just happened* and *it didn't mean anything*

Hello, I'm visiting the area on behalf
of Amnesty International

The world's a pretty scary place and sometimes it seems hopeless,
but it's good to try and make a difference . . . I say my piece
to the twins in sloppy jumpers and blue jeans who answered the door
of their tall, odd house at the top of the hill, but fluff my rhythm
when they swap an honest, amused look and toss their fringes,
each moving her arm on the banister, and I can't help but think
about the long, intimate evenings this September when they sit
on the floor of their blue bedroom, one sketching faces she dreamt,
the other listening on headphones to dead singers from the seventies
while their father, a professor of classics, marks PhDs in his basement
– imagine the suppers of salad and lasagne we could share
in the dim kitchen, the girls showing me their mother's drawings
who died gifting the world with these warm and witty sisters
who'd give anything to know her, and still bake a pink cake
for her birthday, while their father smiles faintly at the paper,
talks of gods and cats, his hands shaking slightly from nerves,
and later I'd take the spare room looking over south-east London,
the park slanted with swings and shadows, the houses staggered
on the hill, where the sun reads from a line of windows, I'd read
till I was tired, and no longer heard the twins' voices in the attic,
their laughter, high and heavy, leaving through the skylight.

Observation of a Neanderthal Colony

This was the first time we'd heard a Neanderthal sing.
We recorded the [mother]'s surprisingly high, clear voice
on two-inch DAT tape as she sang the [children] to sleep.

She washed in the pool and continued to sing, stiffening
a moment before our night-vision cameras detected
the shapes of two large [men]. Both full-grown,

they wore long manes, resplendently black. Their eyes
flared green in our monitors, our microphones picked up
choking sounds in their throats when they approached.

She kept singing as they knuckled her to the ground.
The [children] continued to sleep as both [men] began to [rape]
her, their scruts bobbing an instinctive, pneumatic rhythm.

After satisfying themselves they stalked out;
it was quiet and still for a long time. Our set lights cast
water-pattern predictions on the cave walls.

Another [man] loped in, older, with lashes of silver
in his mane. We recognised the [father]. Finding the [mother]
exhausted and prone, he stroked her back and nuzzled

her neck with a tenderness we found moving.
He turned her over, sniffing her breasts and genitals
where the hair was matted with semen. Quickly,

he became aroused. His penis swelled and reddened;
he tossed her onto her front and mounted, panting audibly.
The [rape] this time was more prolonged, lasting perhaps

ten minutes. Towards his climax, the [father]
pushed the [mother]'s head into the shallow green pool
and held it under. It was difficult to tell if this was deliberate.

Paris

In the middle of that storm-run summer
you met a blind girl in a bookstore.
Her fingers smoothed the patterns
on the spines, as you reached out
and touched her unkempt curls.

In a nearby park, her kisses were precise
as pinches. When you placed a hand
on her hip, or rib, or ankle, her eyes
flickered, forgetful as the fountains,
and each quick motion was your measure.

For a whole week you dreamed
through falling bells and passing birds
of a tall building overlooking churches,
so high your stomach lurched
and the ground reached up with its dumb wish.

Just once she stayed. Outside, cars sighed
and shades of rain contained the room
where her restless gaze reread the ceiling,
each saccade stopped short and repeated,
catching on what, you'd never understand.

Love Story

'Sometimes, doesn't this feel just like
a scene from a book . . .' We sat together
in the cathedral grounds, spoiling novels we loved.

'Not often. If this, say, was written,
every piece would have its purpose,
a reference to call back to, or from. For instance

the part you just described, when the boy on the bus
kept meeting your eye, and you got off a stop later,
met him walking back, and went round his flat

to watch experimental films he made in Manchester
that winter, and you kissed, even if it wasn't lasting
or serious. That would mean something, be deliberate, placed.'

Though it didn't, and it wasn't, I almost added.
The story worked by wanting – we sent ahead,
from the start saw our destination,

the last stop, want returning on a bus top.
I met it, passing me on the way back,
already writing – what . . . 'Sam, I know you'd never do that.'

Back in the Green Night

That year we followed him everywhere,
trekking damp plains, creaky fields of frost,
brown jungle, dim and hazy with spore.
He never noticed us – the exuberant host,
he'd turn from plaiting vines, foot planted on a rock,
for an awestruck aside, or to ask if we were lost
and brandish his trademark deprecating smirk.
He met our lenses only for an instant,
then something from his mind would click
out of his eyes; for hours he'd be vacant.
We lurked behind him like a pack of dogs,
remaining quiet the rest of the descent
while he boomed authorial monologues
at the passing forest, as dull as it was dense.
At camp we marked the map, rubbed our legs
with balm. A guide of long experience,
his wife cooked stews, pitched brocaded tents.
(He won her in duels and endurance tests
years earlier, from an island tribe of innocents.)
Nightlong, he'd demonstrate his skill and vigour
as a lover; nightlong we lay and listened
to her strange cries, saw the sheets mudded with gore
she rinsed and hung up the next morning, like flags
baring their bloods, the terms of her surrender.

There were three of us – me with the camera,
Eddie on lights, McGee did sound and props.
A crack team, our gear bore his insignia.
It's over ten years since the crew split up
but today suburban birches shiver, bring
that same wind through their branches; its slip-

stream enters my blinded room, curls like a finger.
Back in the green night. I'll tell it all,
when in the muggy dark the roused trees ringed us
with their roaring. One wet day he fell,
slipping on a rainslicked root outside a ruin.
His grip sunk an inch in mud, he didn't yell
but mouthed *help* before the ground gave in
and McGee hefted his boom, I started rolling,
saw him bounce from rocks, jerk and spin
down the slope as if on wires. We kept on filming
then made our way to camp, the sleeping lizards
like pale lamps in the trees, the monkeys calling.

Woods panned in one long shot, the river steamed
like tea, and his wife stood for a steady moment
as if this was something she'd already dreamed,
and stared, not seeing us or our equipment.
We tightened the frame, closing in to catch
the slightest change. The moon sparked on my lens
and she was gone; the dark reached out and snatched
her back, like something sprung – she didn't run,
I checked again, just the daze left when a match
has burned. There was little to do but come home then,
and a decade on I still have the reel, a fan's hum,
a plane's faint drone, these windows stopped with sun.

Walter's Excerpt

Such as the instance recently, when Walter
found himself in want of company,
and later found himself at Frick's, a dive bar
on the freeway, its saloon doors head-lit
by prides of trucks. There was a bar girl,
Beulah, with the limp of a straggler,
her excellent back criss-crossed with straps,
who Walter sweetly cajoled into cabbing home
and mixed gins for, and attacked, in the nicest way.

Having lost her earrings, raked his back to ribbons,
Beulah rose, her Bambi lashes dewy with sweat,
passed her drink-froze gaze over the room,
and decided on dislike. The reptiles were first,
bullied with stiletto spikes, then it was Walter's books
that drew her hexes. She stood before them scowling
as Walter groped for weapons. Then she simply
sighed, *It ain't honest to multiply your life like that.*

No Pity

She has ordered quail, and probes the shreds of
     rich meat
from between the nest of bones
until the meal becomes two heaps.

Don't believe you're not dissolving
with the blue light of her bedroom
in a good clean smell of steam,

but maybe you could keep the prod of her hips,
the broken sound her bed makes,
the dark marks of her nipples through her top?

When does it stop being *quail*?
It's hopeless, but at some point there's less
than any one word says. By such patient extractions

even this is cleaned of meaning.
Sun licks mist from the windows,
the restaurant is as bright and tedious

as heaven. You have been reading
how the blessed feel no pity for the damned,
who anyway desire their punishment.

Myself Included

Once I thought experience was everything.
I went round saying it – 'A good experience,
that's the main aim.' It sounded wise
and you could say it in any situation,
in fact a bad one was often best.
After having an experience
I held my breath, searching my reflection
for signs of depth and strengthened character.
It was reasonable proof that I existed
and I once noticed a new line open
at the side of my right eye. My eyes
were very beautiful; sometimes I'd get distracted
and gaze into them all afternoon.

This was before I stopped trusting my opinions,
and went round saying it – 'I no longer
trust my opinions. They are unsafe.'
Sometimes I also said 'I am surrounded
by the dead.' But I'd quickly smile and add,
'Not really . . . !' I began to doubt
my reflection's authenticity –
it didn't blink, and raised a right hand to my left.
Film was an improvement, at least
in terms of accuracy. I filmed my face for hours,
then played it back, filming my face
while watching it. It was hard to read me
as I didn't much react. Also, the silence
of the flat was thickening to fizzy soup,
and I thought I might start hearing voices.
Things were finally getting interesting
but it was time for my trip to America.

It was there I stopped believing
in the value of self-image and experience.
I went round saying it – 'I have no self-image
and have destroyed all my experience.
Also, I am surrounded by the dead
who speak to me through silences
on tapes.' Americans believe such things,
so I'd add, 'Not really!' very quickly.
On the plane I thought about Tom Cruise,
how easily I could visualise his face.
I wondered if his face was a fair gauge
of where and who he'd been, and to what extent
it was the sack his soul was pushed into.

In America I became preoccupied with style
and came up with a great idea for a website
for people who do not trust their opinions.
In New York, the style was that the sidewalk
was too hot to stand on, and postures of the people
attested this. The style of coffee in Chicago
was 'stale lake'. All this came naturally
while I was in America, which proves
how important it is, in terms of style.
I went round saying it – 'America is an important place,
as far as style goes, that is! Now,
would you like me to channel your ancestors?'
I stopped adding the 'Not really!' bit
as my sense of humour was becoming more *acerbic*.
I wondered if this had to do with my loss of opinions
but didn't worry much about it
because I had gone west and now had seen the Pacific Ocean
which looked like an enormous grey car bonnet
bearing down at you. The style of firemen in San Francisco
on Saturdays was to play ping-pong, and the style
of burning houses on Saturdays was to burn with tall red flames

like sheets flying out of windows. By now my forearms
were a beautiful brown colour and I was getting
many admiring looks on the street. I finally convinced myself
of the ocean, closing my eyes and reciting a list of superlatives.

I called Ed about my website. I'd hit on a name
imokareyouok.com, and he'd know if I was onto a winner.
I kept quiet about the dead, however, who I was seeing
more or less constantly, lurching on stairwells
or wading out of subways like someone doing the escalator
party trick, accompanied always by a buzz of flies.
Still, I'd bought ten pairs of shades and was accessorising well
with white sneakers and dark jeans, and the sun glanced often
from the tops of blocks. I watched a girl walk down Polke
with headphones in, like something out of a dance routine.
She cupped her hip as if palming a peach, and I thought,
'What upmarket dream of herself keeps pace with that saunter?'
Her mind was tight as a fist. I resisted the urge to ask,
or tell her how many corpses were dragging themselves
by the lips behind her. Also, I'd started to wonder about Hallowee

It was time to leave. I slow-waved to citizens
from the yellow taxi, but my sentiments were short-lived –
I was frisked at check-in by a fat Hawaiian
when I asked to keep a copy of my fingerprints.
I felt sure I'd unlock the mysteries of my experience
from those soft-looking whorls and grains. As it was,
they told me very little. As it was, the guard scowled
as with prejudice he applied his pocket Maglite to the scar
on my brow. I quailed in his Ray-Bans. 'The scar is a story in itself
I reasoned, failing to placate him. Not that it mattered.
As it was, I was leaving the country, and my thick-necked friend
patted my ass with his torch-butt by means of farewell.

Back in England I decided to avoid all mirrors.
I had been to America, so I went round pretending
I had been to America, with my photos, my new clothes
and everything. 'The *States*', I sneered. But
I needed more than that to convince me. Ed called.
It was no surprise to hear the website was doing well.
I lost my tan fast. I rotated my shades and held my grin.
I'd seen the dead. I didn't miss my opinions much.
One Wednesday night I met Astrid in a restaurant.
She'd been my girlfriend, but we'd separated
due to her view of relationships as arbitrary constructs
and my inability to counter this. 'I like the new style!' she said.
'Thanks,' I responded, 'I'm going for the Clark Kent at college
look and I'm glad you like it.' The stupid bitch didn't realise
I could have said 'the exchange student in '89 look,
thanks for noticing' and it wouldn't be less right.
She knew nothing of the dead – this was obvious
from her flushed complexion and air of well-fed-ness.

At the next table, a fireman and a man in a business suit
covered in blood were sharing a can of 7 Up.
I thought of Tom Cruise, and slipped away
when she'd gone to the Ladies'.
It was getting hard to call, and besides
I felt I'd proved my point. As it was,
I wanted to get back to my flat and my film.
As it was, I hadn't tasted my food.
Outside I looked at all the parked-up cars.
I had made a decision, but based on what?
'This is indicative of a general trend,' I told myself.
I would go around saying it. I wouldn't mention the dead.

At Dilham

I can't remember if we ever met,
but this is the house of my uncle, the poet.
I come here, now he's twenty years dead,
and his son pours wine, measures up my dose of blood.
In his library, I sit alone and pick my nose
at the architect's desk. I read the poems.
A tiny insect crawls on the page, turning *l* to *f*.
Trying to touch him is like pinning down
the point just read. The walls seem deaf
beyond the book, I lilt with drink and sun,
and he's stepping always to the line ahead
before I reach it, his light tread
steady in the metre, so by the end
all's flown to white, I can't turn and find
what I've missed, not quite. *He wrote these in his twenties,*
a POW, and younger than you. It's weird I guess,
this concern with age, with blood and heritage.
The room grows dark, and now the common
thread seems gone, his line
retreats in cold light on the page.
I come back to my own shallow, shifting time,
to life I know, that's warm,
though drink and sun are just the same.
In that sense I suppose he's right, he'll not follow
sons or nephews here. Still, the window
frames the lake, a rain cloud splits
as sunlight hits its sudden edge,
and where the wood he planted knits
its bristle to a shady alphabet,
the deer, unseen, are startling the foliage.

The Aquarium

How long do you stand there
in light bent by its emptiness
where water lies about its depth
and everything is edged with ultraviolet
watching the bass span lazy ellipses
and through a gap in their orbit
the great shark's muzzle
its slow bulk turning like the core of an engine
with all the awful mass and torque
of the ground-zero thought
that keeps the other thoughts moving.